THE ABRAHAM PATH:
A PHOTOGRAPHIC IMPRESSIONISM JOURNEY

VOLUME II

Joshua N. Weiss, Ph.D.

Earle B. Weiss, M.D.

2022

<u>THE FRIEND</u>

Follow the breeze
I know not where I go
I listen to the ripples of time
The stars, my guide ... the sand, my burden
Every breath has purpose
Steps carry ... and confuse me
I persist through a dream
I believe, I trust, I forge ahead
Many will come, but there will be only one true friend

Joshua N. Weiss

<u>DEDICATION</u>

TO THOSE WHO STRUGGLE FOR HUMANKIND.

INTRODUCTION

The origin of this modest volume began in late 2003 when Dr. William Ury and a group of colleagues involved in negotiation and conflict resolution were meeting at a time the United States was involved with the Iraq war. The issue of improving understanding between the core values of the West and the Middle East arose. After considerable discussion the consensus notion of an influential 'bridging' figure who would serve to connect these disparate Western and Middle East worlds might be valuable; that critical figure emerged as the patriarch Abraham/prophet Ibrahim.

At Harvard University, the plan of a Path following the route of the epic journey by Abraham some 4,000 years ago took shape. Its goal in providing a geo-historical route through the Middle East was to foster a greater and more intimate understanding between western visitors and the culture and peoples of that region.

As such, all participants retracing these ancient footpaths would in some measure lead to a greater respect for each other's values. Respect for human diversity that could foster peaceful attitudes represented the philosophy of this undertaking.

Since 2008, thousands of visitors have travelled portions of The Path. Attracting peoples from diverse walks of life, the beneficial sense of communal interest and respect has been exemplary. The path is alive: human antiquity, foundations of major religions, local culture and customs, and one of the most varied geographically diverse and exciting settings on this fragile planet!

This book is another coming together. In recent years my father has rendered photographic images of people, places, and landscapes (1)(2). One day as I was looking over images of the Abraham Path I thought he would like to see them. He had always been interested in the Abraham Path, but from a distance. A few days after sharing that link with him, he called me and suggested this very book - where he would render impressionistic images and I would provide titles and captions. I was very excited to hear the idea and thrilled to work on such a project with my father.

I am forever grateful for the Abraham Path ... And this book is one more example of why.

Joshua N. Weiss (with my father's blessing)

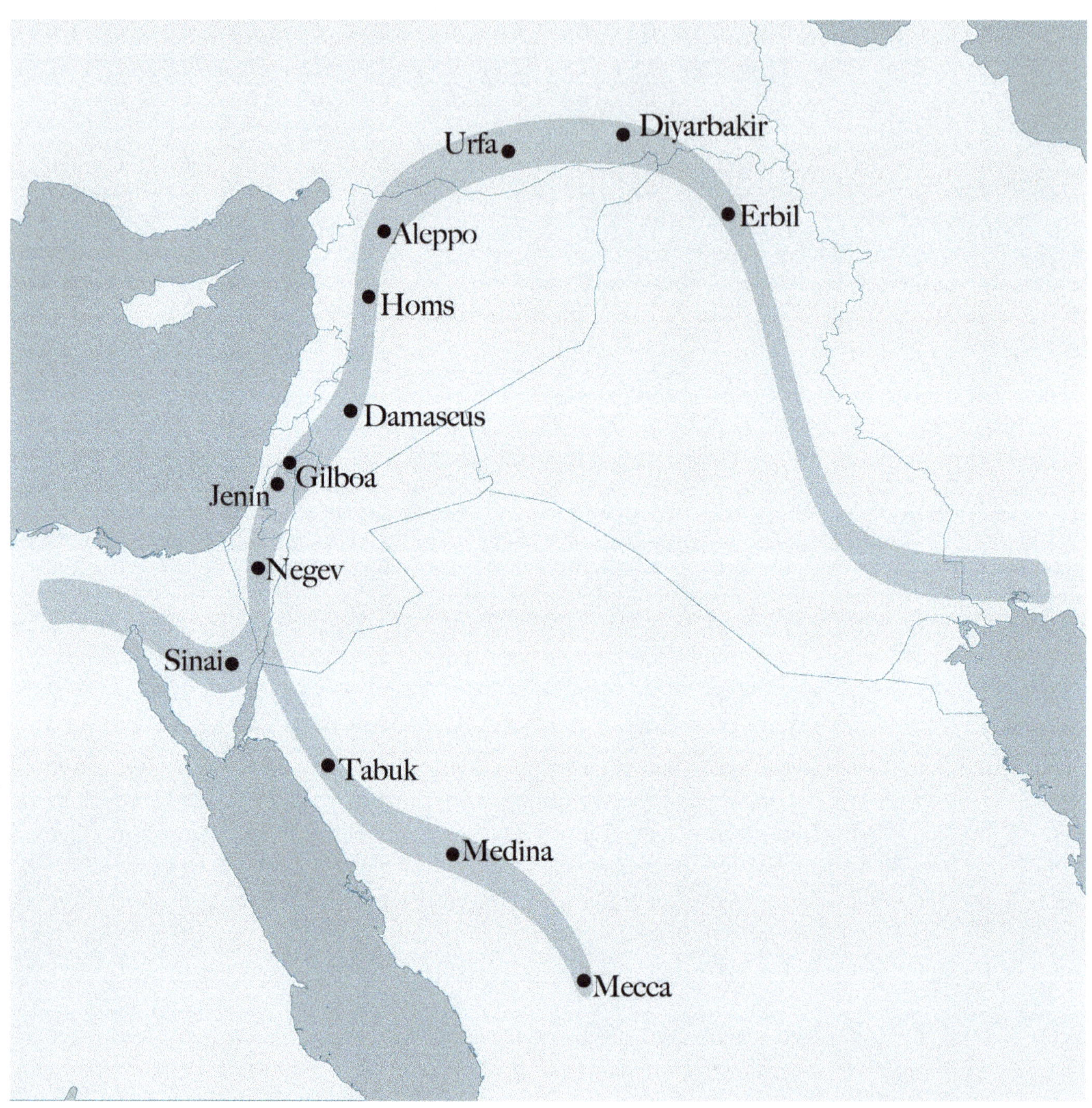

Diyarbakir
Urfa
Erbil
Aleppo
Homs
Damascus
Gilboa
Jenin
Negev
Sinai
Tabuk
Medina
Mecca

<u>HOW THE BOOK IS ARRANGED</u> (3)

The book is organized along the route of the wanderings of Abraham and his family, beginning in the north near Urfa, and ending south, in the Sinai. (4) Please note that some of the names of the places in the captions, particularly the smaller villages, do not appear on the map above but are nonetheless, presented in geographical order. The images capture peoples, historic sites, and landscapes found along The Path.

Another way to view The Path is that of an open-air museum or university.

We hope you enjoy reading through this book as much as we did creating it.

Joshua N. and Earle B. Weiss

<u># A VERY BRIEF RECAPITULATION OF THE STORY OF ABRAHAM (5)</u>

The story begins in a small village some 4,000 years ago. (6) A young boy named Abram (whose name means 'high father') lived there with his family. This boy was a little different. He did not adhere to conventional wisdom about how the world worked. In his time, people believed in many gods and worshipped idols. Equally importantly, there were many unexplained things about the world that very few people questioned. But Abram did. As he gazed upon the stars in the evening he thought there had to be more to the story.

One day when he was tending his family's flock of sheep he heard the voice of God speaking to him. That voice told him there was only one true God and He needed Abram to be His messenger. The voice also told him to go forth into the unknown. Abram did not know where he was to go, only that he should leave his village and their way of life behind and start anew. He packed up his belongings and left with his flock of sheep, his wife Sarai (whose name means 'my princess'), and his nephew Lot, and a few others. They set off for a long, arduous journey and eventually came to rest in Harran in Southeastern Turkey.

After being there for some time God spoke to Abram telling him to go forth toward the land of Canaan and He would make him the father of many nations. After Abram's covenant with God his name was changed to Abraham (which means 'father of a multitude') and his wife Sarai's name was changed to Sarah (which means 'mother of nations').

Many subsequent years of wandering took Abraham to the land of Canaan and beyond - finally settling in the Negev desert in the small village of Beersheva. There he lived out his days and became the father of three great religions: Judaism, Christianity, and Islam.

CONNECTING THE STORY OF ABRAHAM TO THE ABRAHAM PATH

The story of Abraham has often been termed by anthropologists as the most widely shared origin myth on the planet. While the story of Abraham is shared by more than half the world's population, it is much more than a story about religion. The story of Abraham is a tale that motivates many to find their true selves. Who are they? What do they believe? And why?

One of the wonderful things about myths is they carry multiple meanings. Myths are open for interpretation and people can use the stories in ways that make sense to them. The Abraham Path follows the journey wherever Abraham went and honors the different narratives associated with the story.

The world of Abraham was clearly different than present day. Gazing at the night sky a sense of a greater meaning beyond simple stars apparently occupied his thinking. What indeed did it all signify? That process slowly led to a new paradigm; one of a single, all-encompassing and compassionate deity - a notion foreign to the multi-idolatry common at that time. Yet it was profoundly unique.

Such perspective required an extraordinary courage and led Abraham to set upon a journey. Indeed an arduous but eventual monumental journey of exploration, and meditation, culminating in an ultimate conceptualization of Monotheism. Such insight and philosophy eventually became the powerful stimulus for the creation of three major religions with a single and unifying common deity.

Integral to the development of the concept of a physical geographic Path of Abraham is a fundamental belief in human hospitality. Vitally important then to Abraham and his family, this personal and communal commitment to hospitality for all in need or who travel arduous paths remains to this day a crucial and vital element to the ideology of The Path. Succinctly, generous hospitality remains continually practiced by the peoples yet dwelling along this momentous path of Abraham's simple but profound journey.

FOOTNOTES

1. Weiss, E.B., Photographic Impressionism. Volume I, II. Baldwin Hill Art, Natick, Massachusetts, 2014.

2. Weiss, E.B., Studies in Photographic Impressionism, Volume I, Ii. Baldwin Hill Art, Natick, Massachusetts, 2016.

3. The authors have been given permission by the Abraham Path Initiative (API) to reproduce all images used herein. The authors are deeply grateful to the API and the following photographers for their photographs: David Landis, Matt Harms, Stefan Szepesi, Aaron Cederberg, Julian Bender, Beata Andonia, Sumaya Agha, Elias Halabi, Leon McCarron, Frist Meyst, Tony Howard and Di Taylor.

4. The geographic area covered is from Urfa to the Sinai only because those are the parts of the cultural route that have been developed to date.

5. When we use the term Abraham herein it refers to the Abraham in the Judeo-Christian tradition, but also Ibrahim in the Islamic narrative.

6. There are different narratives from the Old Testament and the Islamic Narratives about where this place was located. The Old Testament talks about the village being in Ur of the Chaldees - most believe it to be in present day Southern Iraq. One of the Islamic narratives puts the village near Urfa in Southeastern Turkey.

Nablus - Welcome

As one walks through the Arab regions the phrase 'Ahlan Wa Sablan' rings out; the literal translation being "you've come to stay with family," welcomes strangers.

Nablus - Illumination

This priest is performing his nightly ritual and prayer. Lighting candles is integral to the service illuminating more than just the room ... it lights the fire in people's imagination.

Nablus - Active Marketplace

On the journey along The Path one encounters diverse peoples.

Nablus - Honest Smile

Invariably, the smiling faces of children.

Nablus - Old Meets Old

The aged in the Middle East have seen much life ... good and difficult. Many of the elderly you meet share stories and anecdotes, a form of oral history passed from generation to generation.

Nablus - Burial Grounds

In the Middle East, many cemeteries in ancient lands serve as an important source for tracing local history.

Outside Nablus - Village Nestled In A Valley

In many valleys surrounding olive groves frame villages containing clusters of homes and temples of worship.

Near Nablus - Monastery At Twilight

Monasteries are singular edifices of meditation, often located in isolated landscapes for solitude.

Near Nablus - Couple In Olive Grove

In various locales marriages are still arranged by families. However, younger people are trending towards more Western views from exposure to social media and other modern influences.

Mar Saba - A Fortified Monastery

It is common to see villages and small towns built into the sides of mountains. This ancient walled architecture served primarily for fortification, but also provided shade from the searing desert sun.

Duma - Blue Beauty

Simple attire can still be elegant. In the Middle East the color blue is often associated with protection, holiness and divinity.

Duma - Keffiyeh

The distinctive Keffiyeh head covering is most closely associated with Palestinian culture. The checkered pattern is believed to have originated in Mesopotamia and represent fishing nets or ears of grain.

Auja - Girls Of The Region

Children in many of the rural villages on The Path tend to the animals, help in the fields, and are taught the traditional culture.

Jericho - Fountain At The Center Of The City

Jericho, a name of renown in the Old Testament, is purported to be the oldest continuously inhabited city in the world.

Wadi Qelt - The Valley Of The Shadow Of Death

St. George's Monastery, tucked into the biblical Valley Of The Shadow Of Death, overlooks a stunning view of stark contrasts reflecting both the beauty and the hardship of the terrain.

Wadi Qelt - Cliff Complex

Built in the 4th Century by desert monks seeking seclusion, St. George's Monastery was constructed around a cave where Prophet Elijah allegedly stayed. In the 5th Century the site was occupied by the Greek Orthodox Church.

Wadi Qelt - Winding Path

Traveler pathways, built with great difficulty under hazardous conditions, scale tortuous terrain.

Jerusalem - Morning Market

Markets, with stalls of food, glassware, clothing, and other items, remain a hub of most cities along The Path. The narrow cobblestone streets are joined by newer roads and passageways, built as towns have grown over the centuries.

Jerusalem - A View Of The Western Wall

The Western Wall was part of the foundation of the Temple Mount. After its destruction later buildings were constructed abutting and surrounding this structure.

Jerusalem - Dome Of The Rock

The Dome of the Rock, with its golden presence, dominates the Islamic holy site on the Temple Mount. The Church of the Holy Sepulcher sits in the foreground.

Jerusalem - Approaching The Western Wall

The Western Wall is all that remains of the Second Temple destroyed by the Romans in 70 CE. It is part of the Temple Mount Complex known to Muslims as Al-Haram Al-Sharif. The area is sacred to the three monotheistic faiths: Judaism, Christianity, and Islam.

Near Jerusalem - Market

A marketplace beneath colorful flags during a local celebration.

Jerusalem - Never Stop Dreaming

Along The Path one finds wall murals with expressions of hope. With the Middle East in almost constant turmoil such art continues to reflect human aspirations.

Near Jerusalem - Ancient Alcove

Doorways in alcoves illuminated by streaming light are finely crafted.

Jerusalem - Outside The Old City, Near The Jaffa Gate

The Old City is comprised of four quarters based on the primary ethnicity of the peoples dwelling within - Armenian, Jewish, Christian, or Muslim. It remains a vital center of the holy city of Jerusalem.

Jerusalem - Red Prayer Rugs

Inside the Dome of the Rock the pattern of red prayer mats is woven into the design of expansive carpeting.

Near Bethlehem - Off To School

School is a major component of children's lives throughout the region, if they can afford to attend. Aided by access to social media, education is slowly changing from classical philosophies to Western-based critical thinking.

Bethlehem - Glowing Nativity

Jesus was said to have been born in a cave located under the current Church of the Nativity. Situated on a rolling hill, the site is visited annually by an estimated two million pilgrims.

Bethlehem - Cloaked Woman

Conservative attire for all seasons.

Near Bethlehem - Blowing In The Wind

Hanging decorations sway in the sudden, shifting winds that are common here.

Bethlehem - Greek Orthodox Clerics

The Middle East is home to many different religious sects, many of which have distinctive rituals and garb.

Bethlehem - A Beautiful Meal

Meals along The Path can be sumptuous, plentiful for travelers, and are often shared with the community.

Bethlehem - Rooftop Vista

Find a higher location from which to view a city. Gazing down reveals the magical tapestry of the many rooftops crossed by wandering streets.

Bethlehem - City At Night

Stairs lead to Manger Square in the heart of Bethlehem; bustling during the daytime, they become empty and relatively silent in the evening.

Near Bethlehem - Simple Wonders

One of the things one notices along The Path is how children play with the most minimal of 'toys'. With a little creativity, old rags are knotted together to become a soccer ball and a bottle serves as a shovel to make a sand castle.

Outside Of Hebron - On The Edge

The architecture of the region conforms to the challenge of the desert and embraces its stark beauty.

Hebron - At Wandering's End

In the heart of Hebron, also known as Al Khalil, lies the Cave of the Patriarchs. According to the Old Testament, this is the final resting place of Abraham, Sarah, Isaac, Rebecca, Jacob, and Leah.

Hebron - Abraham And Sarah's Tomb

Along with Abraham and Sarah, a number of prophets and their spouses are interred here.

Hebron - Ancient Terracing

Around the city of Hebron sit many terraced villages and towns. Terracing, which began in the region some 2,000 years ago, enables the use of hilly areas for farming while preventing erosion.

Hebron - The Path Continues

Walking The Path is a literal trek through history. It is often said that the rocks and trees tell their own story of regional events over thousands of years. One just needs to listen carefully!

Hebron - Pastel Enigma

Hebron lies just at the outskirts of the Negev Desert and was once an important way station for ancient travelers and traders. To the southeast lies Beersheva where many people settled because of a nearby aquifer.

Near Hebron - Walking Through The Olive Grove

Along The Path families can be seen walking the land, both to work it and to enjoy its beauty.

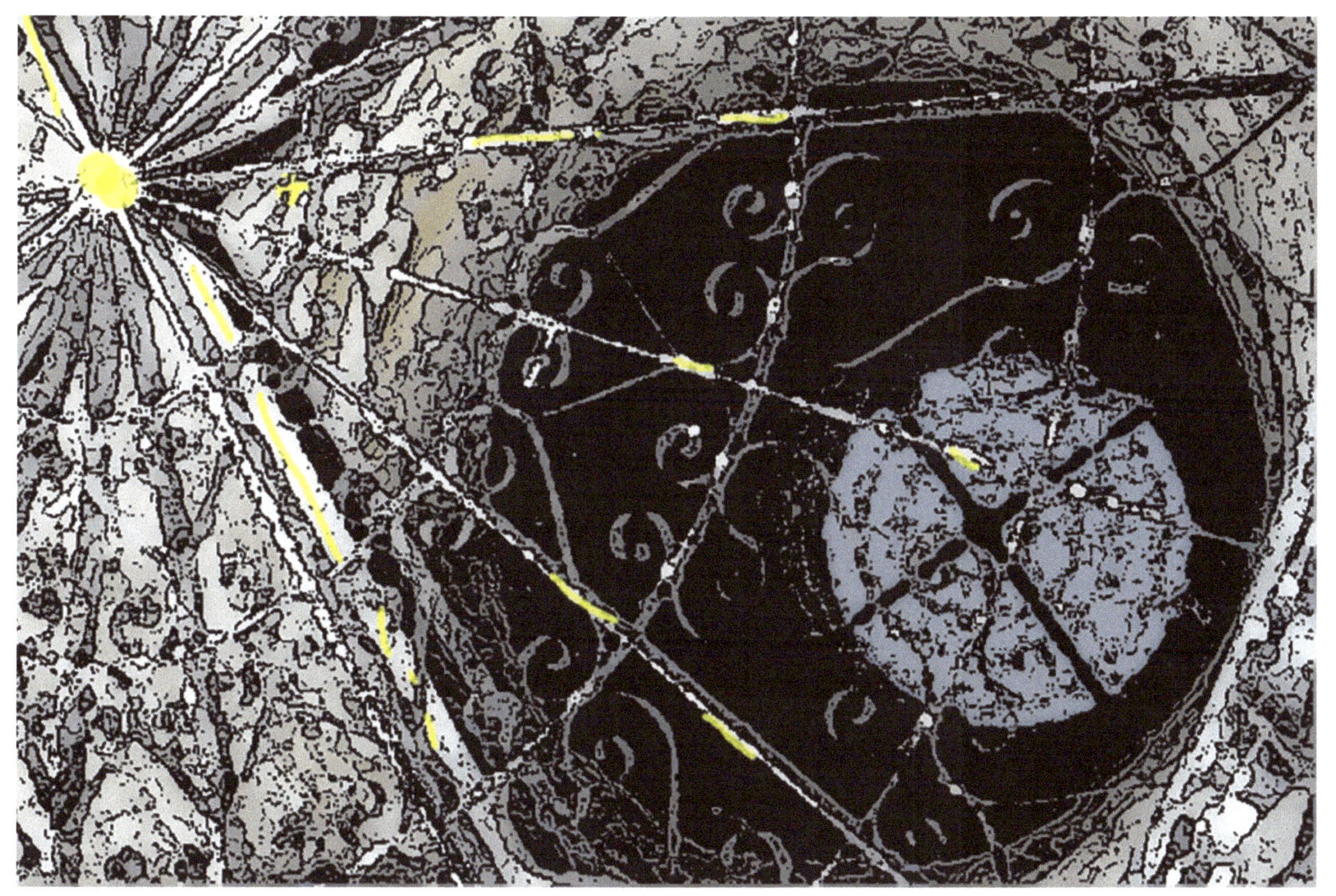

Beersheva - Abraham's Well

Located in Beersheva, where Abraham and Sarah settled after years of wandering, this revered well is a key landmark in the story of Abraham.

Lakiya - Weaving

The craft of weaving continues as an integral part of culture in the Middle East.

Lakiya - Big Boy

A timeless relationship: father and son,

Arad - Desert Bloom

Plants adapt and flourish despite the challenging ecology of the austere desert. Even the brief periods of flowering help sustain life, providing forage for herbivores or seeds for birds.

Near Arad - Nomadic Home

Bedouin life is characterized by a nomadic existence, shifting their locations depending on seasonal conditions or for trade.

Mitzpe-Ramon Negev - Ibex Sunset

Herds of Nubian Ibex, a type of wild goat found primarily in dry mountainous areas, subsist mainly on grasses and leaves.

Southern Negev - Desert Path

Mountains can have a searing beauty, often experienced only by walking, which revels their majesty.

Negev - Mule Rider

The sturdy mule or donkey can trudge long distances carrying loads without difficulty.

Red Sea - Where Mountains Meet The Sea

The Red Sea, which touches Israel, Egypt, Jordan and Saudia Arabia, is crystal clear and warm, providing respite from the desert.

Sinai - Ships Of The Desert

There are still many parts of the Middle East that can only be reached by traveling on camelback.

Sinai - Desert Breakfast

A typical breakfast for the Bedouin is tea and Khoubiz bread. To make Khoubiz a pit is dug and wood burned to coals. Dough is laid on top of the hot coals, then covered with sand. When finished the loaf is struck with sticks to remove adherent sand.

Sinai - Around The Next Corner

The landscapes on The Path include many dramatic vistas, sometimes encountered suddenly along the torturous trails.

Sinai - A Land Of Contrasts

The landscape offers very diverse experiences. Encountering mountains one feels infinitesimally small. Upon ascent one gains a different perspective - the majestic auras of breathtaking views.

Sinai - Challenging Crevasse

There are many crevasses in the desert formed by rushing waters and wind-blown sands, thus creating awesome natural sculpture.

Sinai - Oasis

Oases, a desert phenomenon, enable life in this harsh environment. They are nourished by underground aquifers, usually quite deep, but rise close enough to the arid surface at some locations for wells or plants to tap the water.

Sinai - Desert Smile

A gregarious desert inhabitant might live a harsh life, but still shows a ready smile.

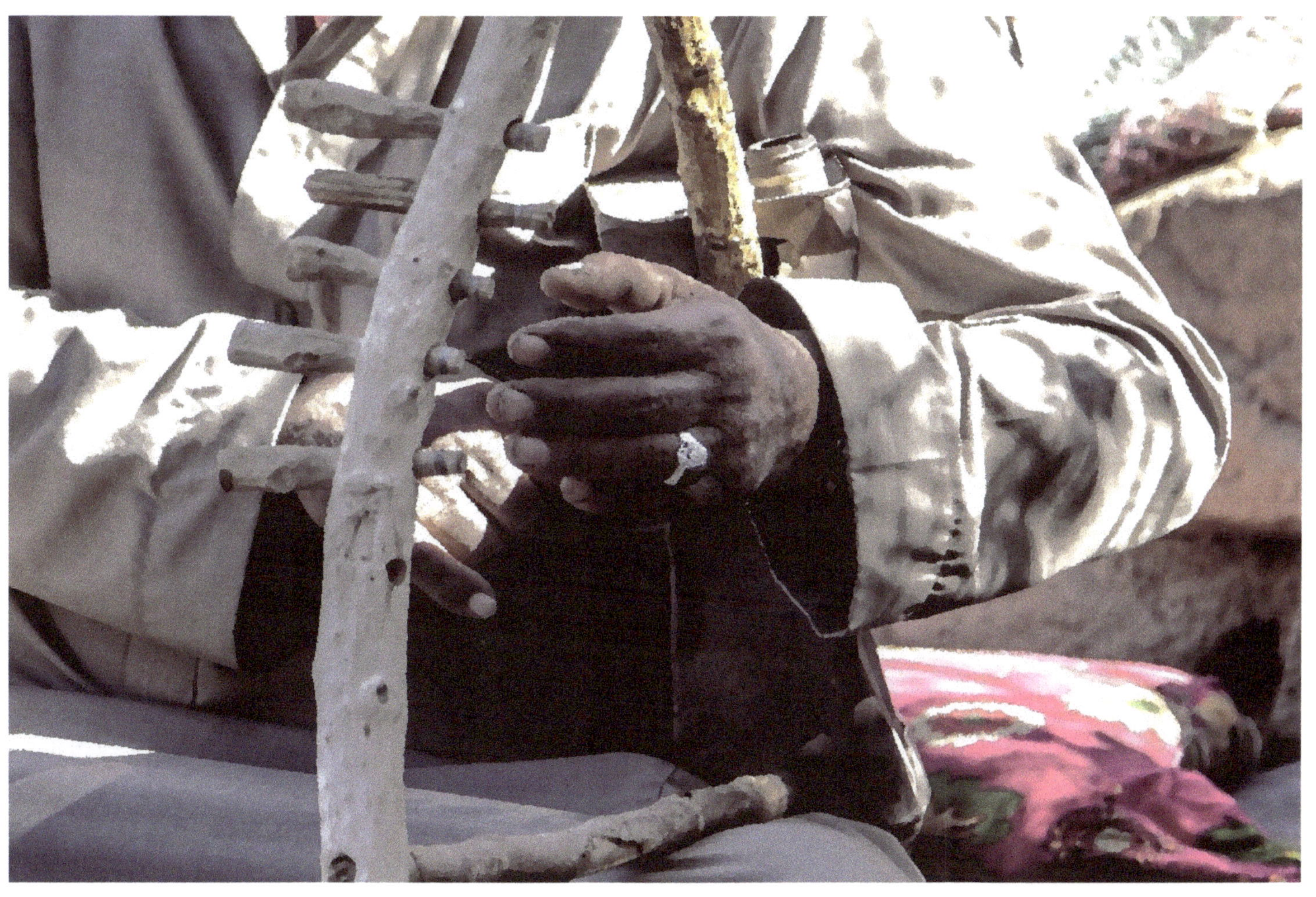

Sinai - Homemade Harp

There are many types of instruments that are found on the Path with the majority, in more rural areas, being homemade. This form of a harp is a common instrument that is strummed and can be tuned with the pegs.

Sinai - Camel Travel

Camels are remarkable animals and can travel over a variety of terrains from deserts to mountains abetted by a good sense of direction. They can drink up to 40 gallons of water per day, storing the fluid in their bodies for many days. Their coats keep them cool from the burning sun.

Mount Sinai - Site Of The Decalogue

Auspicious Mount Sinai has a very distinct topography. Half way up the mountain there is a plateau where water pools allowing plants to survive. Beyond is a relatively steep climb to the summit, aided by steps built by a nearby monastery.

Mount Sinai - Shelter Of Moses

This structure was built on the top of Mount Sinai in honor of Moses. The site is allegedly where Moses spent his days and nights awaiting God's bestowal of the Commandments.

Sinai - Breathtaking Mountains

When viewed from a high location the Sinai is anything but flat desert, rather it consists of mountainous topography punctuated by vast open spaces.

Sinai - God's Vista

The depicted setting is often dramatic near arid areas, highlighting the vast and rugged terrain. Desert dusts create a variety of pastel hues, unique to the region and highly inspiring for visitors to this beautiful land.

www.ingramcontent.com/pod-product-compliance
Lightning Source LLC
Chambersburg PA
CBHW040150110726
48005CB00018B/2712